A S~~OLDIER'S LIFE IN~~

VIKING TIMES

A SOLDIER'S LIFE IN

VIKING TIMES

Fiona Corbridge

FRANKLIN WATTS
LONDON•SYDNEY

Illustrations by:
Mark Bergin
Giovanni Caselli
Chris Molan
Lee Montgomery
Peter Visscher
Maps by Hardlines

This edition 2009

First published in 2006 by Franklin Watts

Franklin Watts
338 Euston Road
London NW1 3BH

Franklin Watts Australia
Hachette Children's Books
Level 17/207 Kent Street
Sydney NSW 2000

A CIP catalogue record
for this book is available
from the British Library.

Dewey number: 355.00948

ISBN 978 0 7496 8870 7

Printed in China

Franklin Watts is a division of Hachette
Children's Books, an Hachette Livre UK
company. www.hachettelivre.co.uk

This book is based on *Going to War in Viking
Times* by Christopher Gravett © Franklin Watts
2000. It is produced for Franklin Watts by
Painted Fish Ltd.
Designer: Rita Storey

Series editor: John C. Miles
Art director: Jonathan Hair

CONTENTS

Lands where the Vikings settled

→ Routes used by the Vikings

● **Major cities**

⚔ *Land battles*

🚢 *Sea battles*

GREENLAND

ICELAND

ATLANTIC OCEAN

NORTH
AMERICA

L'Anse aux Meadows

NEWFOUNDLAND

*King Alfred
of England
won battles
against the
Vikings*

THE VIKINGS

The Vikings lived in Norway, Sweden and Denmark. They were a warlike people who often fought each other. They also attacked and stole from people in other countries.

The Vikings were brilliant at building ships. Warriors (soldiers) used these ships to sail on raids to steal gold and other goods. Some Vikings were traders. They sailed to other lands with animals, timber, furs and slaves to sell.

Viking world
In the eighth, ninth and tenth centuries CE, Viking warriors and traders left Scandinavia and went all over the world.

Eighth century – raids on England and Ireland
Viking warriors started to raid England and Ireland. The English did not win a battle against them for 100 years.

Ninth century – raids on Europe
Vikings attacked trading centres in Europe. They sailed up rivers in France and Germany to get there.

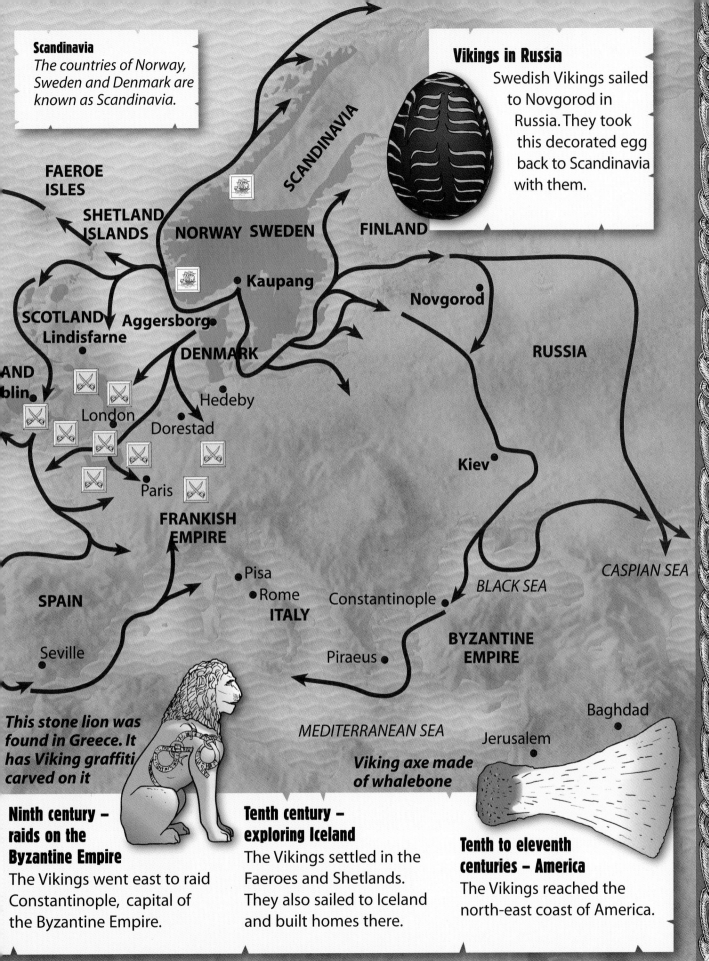

Scandinavia
The countries of Norway, Sweden and Denmark are known as Scandinavia.

Vikings in Russia
Swedish Vikings sailed to Novgorod in Russia. They took this decorated egg back to Scandinavia with them.

FAEROE ISLES

SHETLAND ISLANDS

SCANDINAVIA

NORWAY SWEDEN FINLAND

• Kaupang

SCOTLAND
Lindisfarne •
Aggersborg •

Novgorod •

RUSSIA

AND blin •

London •
Hedeby •
Dorestad •
DENMARK

Kiev •

Paris •
FRANKISH EMPIRE

Pisa •
• Rome
ITALY

Constantinople •

BLACK SEA

CASPIAN SEA

SPAIN

Piraeus •

BYZANTINE EMPIRE

Seville •

This stone lion was found in Greece. It has Viking graffiti carved on it

MEDITERRANEAN SEA

Viking axe made of whalebone

Baghdad •

Jerusalem •

Ninth century – raids on the Byzantine Empire
The Vikings went east to raid Constantinople, capital of the Byzantine Empire.

Tenth century – exploring Iceland
The Vikings settled in the Faeroes and Shetlands. They also sailed to Iceland and built homes there.

Tenth to eleventh centuries – America
The Vikings reached the north-east coast of America.

VIKING WARRIORS

When Viking warriors (soldiers) went into battle or went on raids to other countries, they needed to protect themselves. They wore armour and carried a shield. Rich Vikings had the best armour. Poorer Vikings probably had to fight in their ordinary clothes. They wore a tunic (like a dress), trousers, and a thick cloak to keep warm.

Axe

Helmet

Cloak

Shield

Cloak pin

Chainmail armour

Tunic

Sword

Leather shoes

⬡ CHAINMAIL ARMOUR
Chainmail was made from thousands of iron rings that were linked together. It was made into a coat to protect the body.

⬡ SHIELD
If a warrior was being attacked, he used his shield to try and stop himself getting hurt by his enemy's weapon. Shields were made from wooden boards covered with leather.

FIGHTING BATTLES

Shield

Two-handed axe

Axe

Spear

Weapons

Vikings had lots of dangerous weapons to fight with – swords, axes, spears and knives. Archers fired arrows from bows two metres tall.

Axes

A two-handed axe was held in both hands. It could easily smash through an enemy's helmet. An ordinary axe was held in one hand.

Spears

Most Vikings carried a spear when they went into battle. A spear was a sharp, pointed blade on a long stick. It could be thrown at enemies, or used to stab them.

An animal's antler carved to look like a Viking warrior

Pommel

Cross-guard

⊞ HELMET

Viking warriors wore a metal helmet to protect the head. It had a long piece at the front to cover the nose. Helmets were either rounded or shaped like a cone.

Double-edged Viking sword

⊞ SWORDS

Viking warriors loved their swords and sometimes gave them names such as Leg Biter. Swords had a long blade that was sharp on one edge or both edges.

⊞ SWORD HILTS

The top part of a sword is called the hilt. The cross-guard helped to protect the warrior's hand. Sometimes the hilt was decorated.

CHIEFTAINS

The Viking people were ruled by lots of chieftains. Each chieftain was in charge of a small area. He had warriors who would fight (and die) for him. The chieftains fought each other to try and get the lands of their neighbours for themselves. By CE 1050, the countries of Scandinavia each had a single king.

THE THING

The important people in a community held a meeting called a Thing to settle arguments and decide other matters. It usually lasted for several days.

A chieftain speaking at a Thing

REWARDS

Viking warriors expected their chieftain to reward them for fighting for him. They wanted to be given land and other goods that were won in battle. If the rewards were not very good, they would go and fight for another chieftain instead. The chieftain's most important warriors were called the *lith*. They lived with him.

FIGHTING DUELS

Vikings often settled arguments by a duel (a fight between two people) called a *holmganga*. The fight would take place on a piece of cloth. If either warrior stepped off the cloth, he lost the duel.

BLOOD MONEY

If someone killed a member of a Viking warrior's family, he could demand money from the murderer to make up for it. This was called blood money.

Fighting a duel

HEROES

Sigurd, a hero of legend

This carving shows a blacksmith making Sigurd a sword to kill a dragon called Fafnir.

Sagas

Long stories about Viking gods and heroes were called sagas. Sagas were eventually written down in manuscripts. Some had paintings like this one.

Viking coin

Wild warriors

The names of some warriors tell us a little about them. Lothbrok Hairy Breeches must have worn rough, hairy trousers. Eric Bloodaxe must have killed lots of enemies with his axe.

A VIKING VILLAGE

People in Viking villages made a living in different ways. Farmers, merchants (traders) and craftspeople were called free people. Peasants (who did not own any land) and *thralls* (slaves) worked for the free people.

In the eighth century, the Vikings started leaving their homes to sail all over the world. Warriors went on raids to fight and steal. Merchants sailed with goods to sell.

Shipbuilders at work

TRADERS

Viking merchants sailed to many foreign ports. They sold walrus tusks for ornaments and boxes, furs for clothing and bedding, wood, amber, falcons and slaves.

A Viking village in Norway

RAIDERS

As well as stealing goods, Viking raiders battled to steal land from other countries. Some Vikings decided to settle (live) in the conquered areas, perhaps because their village was crowded, or because they wanted new land to farm.

SETTLERS

Viking men and women settled in England, Orkney and Shetland Islands, the Isle of Man, Iceland, Greenland and northern France. They built homes and raised families. Sometimes they traded with people living nearby, and sometimes they fought them.

A longship

A raiding party gets ready to sail

Planks to surface the road

Animals and people lived close together

LONGSHIPS

Viking warriors went to war and on raids in ships called longships. These were very strong and could also be used for long journeys to explore other lands. The largest longships were 28 metres long and carried 200–300 warriors. Many longships had a scary carved figurehead on the front in the shape of a dragon's head or mythical animal.

Longships were shallow and could sail close to the shore

INSIDE A LONGSHIP

A longship had one large sail to catch the wind. If the wind dropped, the warriors used oars to row with. If the weather was bad, they sheltered in a tent on the deck. There were no seats, so when the men had to row, they sat on the chests that held their personal possessions.

BUILDING A LONGSHIP

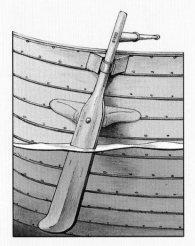

Steering
The ship was steered by a helmsman. He used a steering oar on the right of the ship. Our word "starboard" (steer-board) comes from this. It means the right-hand side of a ship.

Hull of a longship

Hull
The hull (outside shell) of a Viking ship was made from overlapping planks. These were fastened by nails or wooden pegs. Gaps were sealed with rope covered in tar. This sort of hull could bend slightly and rough seas would not damage it. The hull was shallow, so the ship could go near the shore without running aground.

Sail
The sail had a long piece of wood at one corner. The crew moved this to keep the sail in the best position to catch the wind.

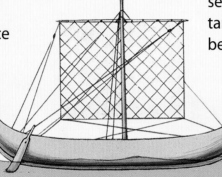

TRADING SHIPS
Ships for trading were called *knorrs*. They were slower than longships. The deep shape of a knorr meant that it could carry lots of things. It could hold goods to trade, or it could take people and animals to new lands.

The Vikings also had smaller boats, which they used for short journeys along the coast of their homelands.

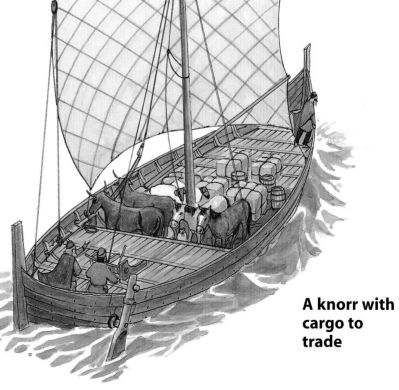

A knorr with cargo to trade

SEA BATTLES AND RAIDS

Viking chieftains often fought each other. They liked to fight sea battles in the sheltered waters of fjords, where it was easy to row the longships. They fixed iron frames to the ships' bows to ram the enemy and put up screens to protect themselves from arrows. Sometimes they tied ships together to make a platform to fight on.

BATTLE OF SVÖLDR

King Olaf Tryggvasson fought a fierce sea battle in CE 1000. His ship, *Long Serpent*, was surrounded by enemies.

Olaf's men tried to leap on to the enemies' ships, but many drowned. In the end, Olaf jumped into the sea and

drowned himself so that he would not be taken prisoner. This battle is described in a saga.

🏵 RIVER RAIDS

The Vikings decided that it was better to raid other countries than to fight each other. They used rivers such as the Rhine in Germany, and the Seine and the Loire in France, to sail inland. They rowed quickly up the rivers, raided towns and left before people could defend themselves.

RAIDS

Attack on Lindisfarne

The island of Lindisfarne in north-east England had a famous monastery. People were shocked when Norwegian Vikings attacked it in CE 793.

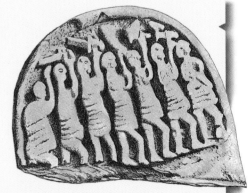

Looters and raiders

Armed Viking warriors attacked poorly defended towns and villages. They also looted (stole) gold and precious objects from churches and monasteries.

Lindisfarne stone

This stone shows Viking warriors waving axes and swords. No one knows who made it. It may have been used on the grave of someone who died in the monastery attack.

LAND BATTLES

The Vikings fought on foot, not on horseback. Their armies were fairly small. Each chieftain kept his best fighters around him.

Battles began with the exchange of arrows, javelins and insults. Then the two sides closed in for a fierce fight.

BANNERS

Each chieftain had a banner or flag that was carried into battle. Many showed a raven, because it stood for the god Odin. The Vikings believed that Odin decided who won or lost a battle.

Defeated Vikings after a battle

BERSERKIRS

Some warriors were known as *berserkirs*. They usually wore a bearskin. They worked themselves into a frenzy before a battle so that they would not feel pain, and fought madly and fiercely. Kings often had berserkirs as their bodyguards. We get the word "berserk" from them.

THE WAY VIKINGS FOUGHT

Shield fort

To defend themselves, warriors sometimes grouped together with their shields to make a *skjaldborg* (shield fort). This protected them until other warriors arrived.

Island camps

When the Vikings went to war, they found that a small island in the middle of a river made a good base for a camp. This was because it was easy to defend against enemies.

Ladders

Sometimes the enemy hid behind banks, fences and walls. The Vikings used equipment like ladders to scramble up to attack the enemy and get inside these defences.

King Alfred of Wessex

KING ALFRED

The Vikings attacked England many times. But in CE 871, King Alfred of Wessex won his first battle against the Danish Vikings at Ashdown. In 878, his army beat them at Edington. This stopped the Danes taking over the whole of England.

Map showing the Danelaw and neighbouring kingdoms

Scotland

Ireland

Welsh kings

Mercia

Danelaw

Wessex

West Welsh

THE DANELAW

When the Danish Vikings couldn't beat King Alfred, they agreed to stay in one part of England. It was known as the Danelaw. The Danes finally conquered England in CE 1014, led by King Cnut.

MILITARY CAMPS

Soldiers lived in a military camp with their families. From there, they would go off to fight. Camps were protected by high earth walls covered with wood, called ramparts.

In Denmark, archaeologists have found fortified camps at Nonnebakken, Fyrkat, Trelleborg and Aggersborg. They were probably built by King Harald Bluetooth.

INSIDE A MILITARY CAMP

The four camps found by the archaeologists were all near a main road. Each quarter of the camp had four long wooden houses built around a courtyard. This was where the soldiers lived.

Soldiers entered the camp through covered gates. Two roads paved with wood crossed the camp.

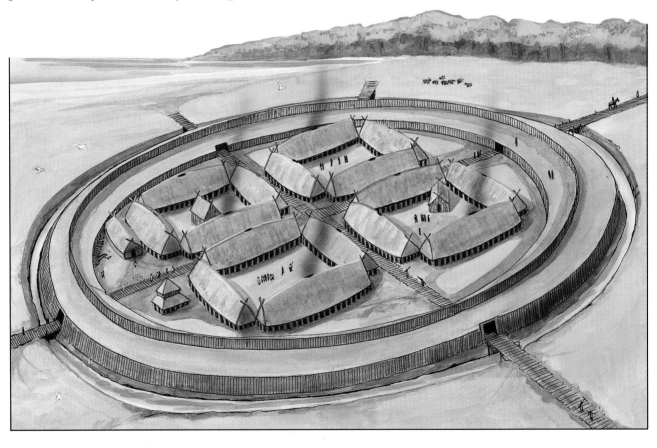

TRELLEBORG CAMP

Trelleborg camp was protected by a large, water-filled ditch and a double wooden palisade (fence). Each of the camp's houses was nearly 30 metres long and had a thatched roof. There was a large living area with a central fireplace. There were also some smaller buildings. Some were used by craftspeople.

VIKING JEWELLERY

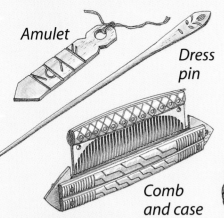

Amulet

Dress pin

Comb and case

Glass beads
Both men and women wore beads. Some beads came from trade with distant lands.

Gold cloak pins

Glass bead necklace

Bone jewellery
Craftspeople carved bone, walrus ivory and antlers to make items such as this amulet, dress pin and comb. The amulet is carved with runes (Viking writing).

Cloak pins
People wore thick cloaks fastened with cloak pins. These were often made from silver or gold and decorated. Men pinned their cloak at the right shoulder so that they could draw their sword easily.

INSIDE A HOUSE
The house had one big room for living and sleeping in. People sat and slept on long wooden benches. In the centre of the room was a hearth where food was cooked over a fire in a large pot called a cauldron. To make fish and meat last for a long time, it could be dried, smoked or salted.

Cauldron over the fire

Hand mill for grinding flour

VIKINGS GO WEST

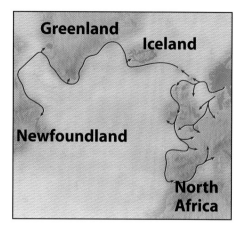

Greenland
Iceland
Newfoundland
North Africa

The Vikings travelled long distances from Scandinavia to raid, trade and settle. They raided England, Scotland, Ireland, France, Germany and the Netherlands. They sailed down to Spain, North Africa, Italy and beyond.

Some Vikings settled in Iceland and Greenland. From here, ships discovered the coast of North America and the island of Newfoundland.

SAILING WEST
In the ninth century, Norwegian Vikings reached Iceland. In the tenth century, Erik the Red sailed to Greenland. His son, Leif, explored the Newfoundland coast.

DANEGELD
Sometimes a king would try to stop the Vikings attacking his country by paying them money. This was called Danegeld. But the Vikings would come back for more.

ATTACKS ON LONDON
London was protected by its old Roman walls (right). In CE 994, Danish Vikings tried to burn the city but failed. In 1016, King Cnut of Denmark tried to capture London. He did not succeed.

ATTACKS ON PARIS

Some towns and cities were protected by ditches or stone walls, but these did not always keep the Vikings out.

In CE 845 a Viking called Ragnar attacked and plundered the city of Paris in France, despite its walls.

In 885–6, a fleet of 700 ships attacked Paris again. Warriors used pickaxes, fire and catapults in the battle.

NORTH AMERICA

Leif Erikson sailed to Newfoundland. He called it Vinland (Wineland) after the huckleberries that grew wild there.

Viking settlers built houses and traded with the Native Americans who lived there. They called the Americans *skraelings* (savages). But before long, fighting broke out between the Vikings and the Americans. After three years, the Vikings decided to sail away.

Native American club with a stone head

VIKINGS GO EAST

As well as travelling west, the Vikings went east. Russia was very close to Sweden, and Swedish Vikings sailed into the country along its rivers.

Other Vikings went south-east as far as Constantinople, the capital of the Byzantine Empire. Here, some of them joined the emperor's bodyguard. They were known as the Varangian Guard.

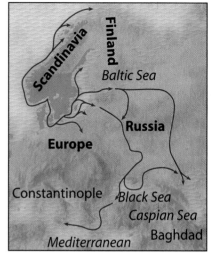

THE BALTIC SEA
Ships sailing to Russia and Finland used the Baltic Sea to get there.

RUSSIAN RAIDS
Swedish Vikings raided Russian towns that were not well defended. In other places, they traded goods. The cities of Kiev and Novgorod became large trading centres.

VIKING HORSEMEN
When Vikings went to other countries, their clothes began to be influenced by the styles that they saw. This Viking horseman's clothes (especially his trousers and tunic) are like those worn by people in Central Asia.

Swedish Viking horseman in eastern-style clothes

TRADE IN THE EAST

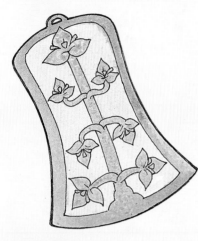

Brazier
A brazier was used to burn charcoal or coal for cooking or heating. Sometimes aromatic spices were burned for their lovely smell.

Silver amulet
Traders travelled all over the East. They brought back things like this amulet, which may have come from Baghdad. It perhaps contained spices.

Bronze Buddha
This statue of Buddha (who founded the religion of Buddhism) was made in India. The Vikings probably used it as an ornament.

RIVER ROUTES

People called Slavs lived along many Russian rivers. Swedish Vikings fought to take control of these communities. The local people called the invaders "Rus". This may be how Russia got its name.

The Vikings used the rivers to sail down to the Black Sea and the Caspian Sea. They went even further to raid and trade. They travelled by foot or by camel to Baghdad, Constantinople and Jerusalem.

Pointed helmet

Stabbing spear

Rus warrior dressed in Central Asian style

Baggy trousers

BATTLE GODS

The Vikings believed in many gods and spirits.

Odin was the god of the dead. He had the power to give victory or defeat in battle. Dead warriors went to live with Odin in his great hall, Valhalla.

Thor was the powerful god of the sky. He protected Asgard, the home of the gods, armed with a mighty hammer called Mjöllnir.

 ASKING FOR ODIN'S HELP
Before battle, a warrior would throw a javelin over the enemy. This was to ask Odin to help him win.

TALISMEN

Hammer amulet

Thor
This figure was made in Iceland in about CE 1000. Thor was said to have a red beard. He was sometimes shown riding in a chariot pulled by goats.

Thor's hammer
Many Vikings wore a hammer amulet, to represent Thor's hammer. They hoped it would give them protection.

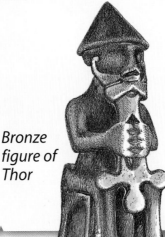

Bronze figure of Thor

Ragnarök stone
This carving is of a huge battle called Ragnarök, in which the gods were killed. Here Odin is being eaten by his old enemy, the wolf Fenrir.

THE VALKYRIE

The Valkyrie were beautiful female spirits who served Odin. Sometimes they wore armour and rode horses over land and sea. They flew over battlefields to choose dead warriors and take them to live with Odin in Valhalla.

SHIP BURIAL

When a Viking chieftain died, he was sometimes buried in a ship. The Vikings believed that this would take him to the afterlife. He was buried with his possessions. Slaves and horses might also be killed to accompany him. Sometimes the ship was burned so that the chieftain would go to the afterlife quickly.

VIKINGS AND CHRISTIANITY

The Vikings were pagans and believed in gods such as Odin and Thor. When they raided Christian countries, they stole from churches and monasteries.

But then some Viking kings became Christians, and so did their people. Denmark became Christian in about CE 960, when Harald Bluetooth was king. Norway, ruled by King Olaf Haraldsson, followed in about 1024. Sweden stayed pagan until the end of the eleventh century.

BECOMING A CHRISTIAN

Once ordinary people realized that their kings were not punished by the old gods for becoming a Christian, they also decided to be Christians. Many fine wooden churches were built throughout Scandinavia.

BAPTISM

The scene from an altarpiece (right) shows a bishop baptizing King Harald Bluetooth of Norway in a barrel. Baptism is the ceremony where a person is sprinkled with water as a sign that he or she has become a Christian.

CHRISTIAN SYMBOLS

Stave church

Wooden churches, like this one at Borgund in Norway, were built from tree trunks split in two (called staves).

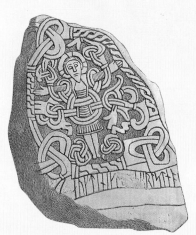

The Jelling stone

After he became a Christian, King Harald Bluetooth put this stone at Jelling in Denmark, in memory of his parents. The stone is the earliest picture of Jesus found in Scandinavia.

Church decoration

Craftspeople carved wooden panels to decorate the stave church at Urnes in Norway. They show ribbon-like beasts biting one another.

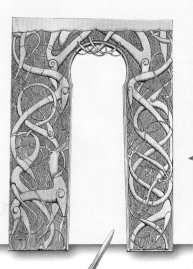

THE NORMANS

In CE 911, a Viking called Rollo was given land in France. His followers were called Northmen or Normans. They learnt French and became Christians. In 1066, a descendant of Rollo won the Battle of Hastings and conquered England. He was called William of Normandy.

KNIGHTS ON HORSEBACK

In the twelfth century, the Vikings began to use the same ways of fighting as the people of Europe. Knights were trained to fight from horseback. They carried long shields instead of circular ones.

Norman knight, a descendant of Viking seafarers

GLOSSARY

Afterlife
The next world, where Vikings believed they went when they died.

Amber
Sap from pine trees that goes solid and is used for jewellery.

Amulet
A piece of jewellery worn to protect against evil.

Archaeologist
A person who studies human history by looking at ancient items that have been discovered, such as bones, the remains of buildings, and possessions.

Berserkir
Warrior who wore a bearskin shirt and fought in a frenzy.

Byzantine Empire
In the third century CE, the Roman Empire was divided into eastern and western parts. The eastern part became the Byzantine Empire. Its capital was Constantinople (Istanbul).

Community
A group of people living together.

Craftspeople
People who are skilled at making certain things.

Danegeld
A kind of ransom paid to invading Danish armies so they would go away.

Danelaw
An area of England where Danish Vikings agreed to stay after making a treaty with King Alfred in 886.

Defence
Protecting a person or place against danger, harm or attack.

Fjord
Long, narrow inlet of sea between high cliffs. It is pronounced "fee-ord".

Fortified
Strengthened. A building is fortified by building walls and fences to protect it.

Franks
A Germanic people who controlled much of western Europe from the sixth century CE. They eventually settled in what we now know as France and Germany.

Knorr
Viking ship with deep sides, for carrying goods and trading.

Legend, legendary
A legend is a story that has been handed down from earlier times. It may or may not be true.

Lith
Group of warriors loyal to their chieftain. They lived with him.

Longship
Slim ship with a shallow hull. It was fast, with a single square sail. It usually had at least thirteen rowers on each side.

Looter
A person who steals money or goods on a raid.

Monastery
A building where a religious community of monks lives away from everybody else.

Myth, mythical
A myth is a story about imaginary (made up) beings or creatures with special powers.

Native American
The original tribal peoples of North America.

Pagan
Someone who has religious beliefs but does not follow one of the main world religions. In Viking times it meant a non-Christian.

Palisade
A strong wooden fence, made of stakes driven into the ground.

Pickaxe
A tool with a pointed metal head and wooden handle.

Rampart
An embankment (ridge of earth or stone) around a fort or military camp, to protect it. It may contain walls or fences.

Raven
A large bird with black feathers and a croaking cry.

Runes
Ancient alphabet used by the peoples of Scandinavia before and during the Viking period. The angular letters were easy to carve on stone and other hard materials.

Sagas
Long stories about the lives and bravery of Viking heroes. To begin with, sagas were told by *skalds* (poets). They were not written down until at least the eleventh century.

Skalds
Viking poets who specialized in reciting sagas and other tales about gods and legendary heroes.

Stave church
An early type of Scandinavian church. To make the walls, logs were split in two and set upright, side by side.

Talisman
A small object carried to protect a person against evil. It was often carved.

Thrall
A slave, often a captive taken by the Vikings in battle or during a raid.

Valhalla
The hall of Odin, the god of the dead. Some dead warriors were taken there to live with Odin. "Valhalla" was sometimes used to mean life after death.

Valkyries
Female servants of Odin who chose which of the warriors killed in battle should be taken to Valhalla to be with Odin. At one time they were feared as demons, but then were thought of as princesses in armour.

Varangian Guard
The Viking warriors who served the Byzantine emperor at Constantinople and formed his bodyguard.

Vinland
"Wineland". The Vikings' name for the area on the coast of North America where they settled. It was probably Newfoundland in Canada. They probably thought the huckleberries that grew there were grapes.

INDEX

><-I-<>-O-<>I->